In *from unincorporated territory* [åmot], Craig Santos Perez sings down healing for the speaker who asks, "isn't that too / what it means to be / a diasporic chamoru // to feel *foreign in your own homeland.*" Each poem probes this question against the continued disenfranchisement and militarization of Guåhan and the CHamoru people. From elegies for loved ones, continual rewriting of prayer, and eating rice with the grandmother, the rituals in this collection bear the histories of family, of the church's spiritual abuse, and of the colonization of the island. But for endurance and renewal there is hope; each poem-story is itself a plant that yields a seed the speaker gathers. Each seed bursts its casing to branch into a meeting place for inter-generational memory and wisdom. What was deemed unworthy, flowers wildly, coded in the name of the plants reclaiming their CHamoru names banking these pages. In this collection Craig Santos Perez's vital poems prove yet again that his necessary and clear voice is one that shakes the foundations of nation and demands of the reader to consider their complicity in the machinations of Empire.

—**Rajiv Mohabir,** author of *Cutlish*

Craig Santos Perez's multi-volume from unincorporated territory is one of the great poetic sequences of our decolonial time, and this latest installation [åmot] is an urgent meditation on dispossession in the face of ecocide and a celebration of poetry's eccentric, medicinal power to counter new and old forms of imperial violence, from military occupation to resource extraction. Against the "latitudes & longitudes / of empire" and its "bleached coral," Perez deploys lyric narratives, family histories, indigenous legends, recipes, hashtags, reading lists, archipelagic calligrams, translingual jokes, (alter)native botanies, and a range of diasporic maps (Spam backwards), so as to center the "aerial roots" that can attune us to "the intertextual / sacredness / of all things." In a small place like Guåhan (Guam), Perez finds the oceanic language for a new kind of book that can "re-wild" the word and the world.

—**Urayoán Noel**, author of *Transversal*

Craig Santos Perez continues to expand visual literacies of Pacific Literature as he grapples with the question: what does it mean to write the ocean? Here are handwoven, blessed nets of intergenerational Chamoru stories. If a poem could unstitch a barbed wire fence, throw net, play bingo, unshipwreck Indigenous youth, care for elders, or heal a broken heart with Spam, that poem is in these pages. Propelled by gratitude, this book is a call to defy and protect, a sea of poetic innovation and care.
—**No‘u Revilla**, author of *Ask the Brindled*

[åmot], the fifth stunning collection of Craig Santos Perez series *from unincorporated territory* combines Guåhan's natural and cultural histories, as well as CHamoru visual and oral literacies, to create a poetic form of healing that Édouard Glissant might have hailed an aesthetic of the Earth. Like the banyan tree that expands and strengthens through aerial roots, the poetry of [åmot] is a "medicinal plant" that seeds from the diasporic roots of Guåhan, from its histories fragmented by imperialisms, from CHamoru ancestors and elders, from the egg of an exiled Micronesian Kingfisher, to radiate back to their center: Guåhan. With this fifth opus, Perez accomplishes a tour de force by literally fusing Guåhan's natural and cultural forms with the poetic fabric, and by mapping a CHamoru ecology of healing, between home and displacement. A literary achievement carried out through lyricism, communality, humor, gratitude, and responsibility.
—**Beatrice Szymkowiak**, author of *Red Zone*

Previously Published Poetry

Habitat Threshold, Omnidawn Publishing, 2020.

from unincorporated territory [lukao], Omnidawn Publishing, 2017.

from unincorporated territory [hacha], Omnidawn Publishing, 2017 (First edition, 2008)

from unincorporated territory [guma'], Omnidawn Publishing, 2014.

from unincorporated territory [saina], Omnidawn Publishing, 2010.

from unincorporated territory

[åmot]

Cover art by Craig Santos Perez

Cover typeface: Garamond
Interior typeface: Garamond Premier Pro

Cover design by Craig Santos Perez
Interior design by Craig Santos Perez and Laura Joakimson

Library of Congress Cataloging-in-Publication Data

Names: Santos Perez, Craig author.
Title: From unincorporated territory [åmot] / Craig Santos Perez.
Other titles: Åmot
Description: Oakland, California : Omnidawn Publishing, 2023. | Includes
bibliographical references. | In English with some text in Chamorro. |
Summary: "This book is the fifth collection in Craig Santos Perez's
ongoing from unincorporated territory series about the history of his
homeland, the western Pacific island of Guåhan (Guam), and the culture
of his indigenous Chamoru people. "Åmot" is the Chamoru word for
"medicine," and commonly refers to medicinal plants. Traditional healers
were known as yo'åmte, and they gathered åmot in the jungle, and
recited chants and invocations of taotao'mona, or ancestral spirits, in
the healing process. Through experimental and visual poetry, Perez
explores how storytelling can become a symbolic form of åmot, offering
healing from the traumas of colonialism, militarism, migration,
environmental injustice, and the death of elders"-- Provided by
publisher.
Identifiers: LCCN 2022057633 | ISBN 9781632431189 (trade paperback ;
acid-free paper)
Subjects: LCSH: Guam--Poetry. | LCGFT: Visual poetry. | Experimental
poetry.
Classification: LCC PS3619.A598 F76 2023 | DDC 811/.6--dc23/eng/20221212
LC record available at https://lccn.loc.gov/2022057633

Published by Omnidawn Publishing, Oakland, California
www.omnidawn.com
10 9 8 7 6 5 4 3 2 1
ISBN: 978-1-63243-118-9

from unincorporated territory

[åmot]

craig santos perez

Omnidawn Publishing
Oakland California
2023

"guello yan guella
kao siña mañuli' yu' tinanum-mu
yanggen måtto hao gi tano'-hu
chule' ha' hafa malago'-mu"

"ancestors, i respectfully ask permission
to gather some of your plants
and if you should come to my place,
please take whatever you need"

Map of Contents

~

"By a glance at the map it may be seen that one quarter of the population of the world lies on a rough semicircle of which the meridian of Guam is the diameter, and Guam itself the center."

—*Guam Governor's Annual Report,* 1915

~

ginen ta(lå)ya
ginen mannginge'
ginen ta(lå)ya
ginen mannginge'
ginen ta(lå)ya
ginen achiote
ginen sourcings
ginen during your lifetime

~

ginen sounding lines
ginen the micronesian kingfisher
ginen sounding lines
ginen the micronesian kingfisher
ginen sounding lines
ginen the micronesian kingfisher
ginen sounding lines

~

ginen sounding lines
ginen the balutan archives
ginen the zen of spam
ginen the balutan archives
ginen the zen of spam
ginen the legends of juan malo
ginen the balutan archives
ginen the legends of juan malo
ginen the zen of spam

~

ginen sounding lines
ginen aerial roots
ginen åmot

ginen aerial roots
ginen åmot
ginen family trees
ginen åmot
ginen family trees
ginen the micronesian kingfisher
ginen åmot

~

ginen sounding lines
ginen ars pasifika

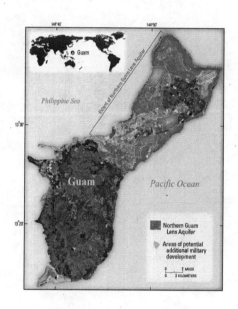

ginen **sounding lines**

~

hasso'
the first map tåta : *dad*
hangs in the hallway
"where's our village" i ask
"here" he points to its center
"mongmong" : *heartbeat*
i read other village names
yigo dededo tamuning
barrigada mangilao chalan pago
ordot toto maite hagåtña
hagåtña heights sinajana asan
piti yona santa rita
agat talofofo umatac
inalåhan merizo
"atan" tåta says
: *look* "this is
puntan's body"

~

[sumak : *randia cochinchinensis*]

15

~

What is #Guam famous for? Did Magellan discover #Guam in
1521? Was #Guam the first Pacific Island colonized by Europeans?
Was #Guam an important stop on the Acapulco-Manila galleon
trade route? Did Spain own #Guam? How many people died during
the Spanish-Chamorro War (1668-1698)? Is #Guam Catholic? Was
#Guam annexed by the United States after the Spanish-American War
of 1898? Did the Supreme Court Insular Cases designate #Guam
an "unincorporated territory"? Did Justice Harlan write in Downes
v. Bidwell: "I am constrained to say that this idea of 'incorporation'
has some occult meaning which my mind does not apprehend. It is
enveloped in some mystery which I am unable to unravel." Is #Guam
home to the indigenous Chamorro people? Are pure Chamorros
extinct? Is it spelled "Chamorro" or "CHamoru"? Did Chamorros
become US citizens after the Organic Act of Guam in 1950? Does
the military occupy thirty percent of #Guam's landmass? Is the
Department of Defense planning a massive new military buildup on
#Guam? Are they constructing a live firing range complex in Litekyan
(Ritidian)? Is Litekyan an ancient CHamoru village with archaeological
remains and a wildlife refuge covering 371 acres of coral reefs and 832
acres of terrestrial habitats? Is #Guam a strategic location? Why do
so many CHamorus enlist in the U.S. military? Is #Guam the tip of
America's spear in Asia? Is #Guam dangerous? Is #Guam a target for
North Korean missile strikes? Is #Guam in danger? What are the top
10 essential facts about #Guam? Does #Guam lie on the other side of
the international date line? Is #Guam "Where America's Day Begins"?
Is #Guam America's westernmost frontier? Do CHamorus watch the
Super Bowl on Monday? Is #Guam the SPAM capital of the world?
What are 5 things you can only do on #Guam? Is Trump using #Guam
as a pawn in his nuclear stand-off with North Korea? Can #Guam vote
for the U.S. President? Is #Guam a tiny island caught in a global war of
words? Was #Guam renamed #Guåhan? Does #Guåhan translate into

we have, as in *we have* so many questions? Is #Guåhan just rhetoric? Did Dennis Rodman visit #Guåhan on a peace mission? Does #Guåhan see this apocalyptic threat as a new tourism opportunity? Is #Guåhan experiencing flashbacks from the Japanese invasion during World War II? Is #Guåhan learning how to survive a nuclear attack? Did the civil danger radio warning startle #Guåhan? Is every inch of #Guåhan targeted by China's DF-26 ballistic missile, known as the "Guam Killer," which was showcased at the Chinese military's 70th anniversary parade in Beijing? Is #Guåhan on edge? Tipping over? Capsizing? Is the whole world watching #Guåhan? Is #Guåhan accustomed to being the center of global attention? Did #Guåhan change after it went viral? Is #Guåhan already forgotten?

[*tapun ayuyu : elatostema calcareum*]

ginen **achiote**
for grandma rose beatrice hughes perez

~

hasso' : *remember* grandma
picks me up after school
from carbullido elementary
in barrigada

"did you win at bingo"
i always ask her

if she did
[we] drive to mcdonald's
for filet-o-fish sandwiches
fries & cokes

if not
[we] go to her house
in toto
& she cooks
hineksa' aga'ga'   : *red rice*

~

hasso' bright yellow
bag of imported calrose rice
in grandma's pantry

      extra fancy   *enriched*

red diamond "g"
which I thought meant "guam"

i scoop three cups of rice
into a pot
she turns on the sink water   *: hà nom hà nom hà nom*

"what does *calrose* mean"
i ask her

"i don't know"
she says
cleaning white grains
with gentle
brown hands

guello yan guella   tell me again

our words for rice

fa'i	: *rice growing in field*
fama'ayan	: *rice field*
timulo	: *harvested, unhusked rice*
tinitu	: *husked rice*
chaguan aga'ga	: *wild rice*
pugas	: *uncooked rice*
hineksa'	: *cooked rice*

guello yan guella   tell me again

how you planted
during fa'gualo   : *october moon*

harvested
with conch shell tools

husked
with lusong & lommok   : *mortar & pestle*

*tell me again   how rice
                was once ceremony*

[*potpupot : peperomia mariannensis*]

ginen **trespass** *[the lord's preyer]*

"The rape of Oceania began with Guam."
—Douglas Oliver, from *The Pacific Islands* (1951)

~

our padre
who art on galleon
1665 : jesuit diego luis de san vitores
convinces king philip iv of spain
& queen maria anna of austria
to fund guam mission
canonized be thy name
thy priesthood come
1668 : san vitores arrives to guam
names archipelago "marianas" to honor
queen mother of spain & virgin mary
thy abuse be done
on guam
1669 : san vitores establishes first
catholic church "dulce nombre de maria"
which was our safe haven
1670 : san vitores baptizes
thousands of chamorus
give [us] back our boys
hundreds of children die after baptism
our altar boys

[pupulun aniti : piper guahamense]

ginen **achiote**

~

i help grandma
deseed the red pods
of achiote plants
growing in her yard

[we] dry heart-shaped seeds
in aluminum trays
beneath the territorial sun

~

she soaks seeds in hånom
pours liquid into pot of cleaned rice

salt boil simmer stir cover

~

guello yan guella   tell me again

how you wrapped rice
in banana leaves
placed in bamboo
filled with hånom
& cooked over guafi   : *fire*

tell me again how rice
was once currency

~

[we] sit across from each other   on the dining table

& play rummy   as rice cooks

i shuffle & deal   [we] take turns

picking cards   from the deck

choose what to keep   what to discard

i was too young to ask her   about japanese soldiers

flooding   i tåno'

our people forced   to grow rice

for their army

all day
in the paddies

beneath
the imperial
sun

bowing

[ahgaga : melothria guamensis]

ginen **trespass**

~

our rey
who art in spain
1672: san vitores baptizes
chief mata'pang's daughter
without permission
sovereign be thy name
thy priesthood come
1767: edict of king charles iii
bans jesuits from colonial possessions
augustinian recollects
supply missionaries to guam
thy abuse be done
on Guam
1807: marianas mission placed under
diocese of cebu philippines
which was our safe haven
1899 : new american governor
naval captain richard leary
orders removal of augustinian recollects
give [us] back our boys
1901: spanish capuchin missionaries
arrive to apra harbor
our sacrificed boys

[mayagas : cassytha filiformis]

ginen **achiote**

~

i was too young to ask grandma
about the march   : *[lukao]*
to the concentration camp
in manenggon *[1944]*

she was 23 years old

~

guello yan guella   tell me again

     how you pilgrimaged   to fouha rock in humåtak bay

gi tinituhon   : *in the beginning*

fu'una
transforms puntan's
back into tåno'   : *land*
chest into langet   : *sky*
eyes into atdao   : *sun*
& pulan   : *moon*

26

~

      i was too young to ask
about bayonets

      relatives   who fell behind

    haga'

           haga'

           haga'

27

~

guello yan guella   *tell me again*

how you made offerings
        to fu'una & puntan

asked blessings for
simiya   *: seed*
hale'
talåya
hineksa'

                    ~

                was
                too young

ask

                how

                many
                months

                pregnant

                                                    (first

                                                    child

                        håga

28

~

guello yan guella   tell me again

       how you stood in circles
& chanted kåntan chamorrita

how fu'una dived into tåsi
       transformed into stone

& birthed us
at laso fu'a   : *creation point*

   ~

too young
to understand

                          "mis-

                          carriage"

                  (wrapped

                  in banana leaves

                  håga   *haga'*

[galak dangkulo : asplenium nidus]

ginen **trespass**

~

our pedophile
who art in rectory
1907: guam removed from
diocese of cebu philippines
placed under spiritual jurisdiction
of prefecture apostolic of marianas
predatory be thy name
thy priesthood come
1914 : guam mission handed over
to capuchins of navarre spain
thy abuse be done
on Guam
which was our safe haven
1965: vicariate elevated to
diocese suffragan of
san francisco archdiocese
give [us] back our boys
our silenced boys

[seiyaihagun : nervilia aragoana]

ginen **achiote**

~

guello yan guella   *tell me again*

how you carried

blessed rice
back to the villages
to feed i famagu'on   : *children*
& i manånko'   : *elders*

~

to ask

how

did you

keep walking

(carrying

haga'

håga

: *blood*

: *daughter*

31

~

when hineksa' aga'ga'
is cooked
grandma lifts
the lid

steam dances
around her face

she fills
our bowls

[we] eat on the porch

i uchan : *rain*

~

guella yan guello
tell me again
how rice was once
åmot
: medicine

tell me again
how to sing
forwards &
backwards

ginen **trespass**

~

our santo papa
who art in the vatican
1981: pope john paul ii visits guam
whose population is 85 percent catholic
higher percentage than italy
trusted be thy name
thy priesthood come
1984: diocese of agana
elevated to a metropolitan archdiocese
thy abuse be done
1985 : san vitores beatified
on guam
which was our safe haven
shrine of san vitores
built in tumon for $350,000
believe our boys
partially funded by guam visitors bureau
& proceeds from liberation day
our altered boys

[kajlao : phymatodes scolopendria]

33

ginen **family trees** *[litekyan]*

"Trees are poems that the earth writes upon the sky."
　　　—Khalil Gibran, from "Sand and Foam" (1926)

　　　　　～

hasso' before [we] enter
i hålom tano'　　　　　　　　　　　　: *deep jungle*
tåta asks permission
　　　　of i taotaomo'na　　　　　　: *spirits*
who dwell within

　　　he closes his eyes
& whispers "ekungok"　　　　　　　: *listen*

　　　～

as [we] walk
he recites the names
of each tree
each elder　　　　　　　　　"niyok"
　　　　　　　　　　　　　"lemmai"
　　　　　　　　　　　　　"ifit"
　　　　　　　　　　　　　"yoga"
　　　　　　"nunu"
who provides [us]
clothes & tools
canoes & shelter
food & åmot

34

~

"when you take"
he says

"take with gratitude
     & never more than
what you need"

    ~

[we] reach the chain linked fence
      crooked *no trespassing* sign
beaches we can't access
      oceanic horizon we can't see

he tells me how the military
uprooted trees
paved i tåno'
planted toxic chemicals
& ordnances

he translates
"eminent domain" as "theft"

to turn places of abundance
into bases for destruction

barb   -ed   wi   -re

        spr   -eads

li   -ke   in-

        va   -sive   vi-

nes   who   -se   on

        -ly   flo   -wers

are   ca   ncer   -ous

        tu   -mors   bl

    -oom   -ing   on   ev

ery   br   -anch   of

    our   fam   -ily   tr   -ee

~

today the military invites [us]
        to collect plants & trees
within areas of litekyan   : *stirring place*
        slated to be cleared
for a firing range   : *what follows your flag*

they tell us
to fill out appropriate forms
        & wait two weeks
for a security check

        if [we] receive *their* permission
        they'll escort [us] to mark & claim
trees [we] want delivered
after removal

they call this "benevolence"

yet why
does it feel
like a cruel
reaping

[*pugua machena : davallia solida*]

ginen **trespass**

~

our pale'
who art in cathedral
1986: anthony sablan apuron elevated
to metropolitan archbishop of agana
defrocked be thy name
thy priesthood come
thy abuse be done
2016 : hundreds of lawsuits filed
against archdiocese of agana & 16 priests
alleging sexual abuse of minors from 1950s to 1980s
on guam as it was elsewhere
2017: church declares year of reparation
sets up organization called "hope & healing"
offering counseling to sex abuse victims
believe our boys
our almighty boys
2018: vatican tribunal finds archbishop apuron
guilty of sexual abuse charges
suspended & ordered not to return to guam
& pay just reparations
as [we] indict those who trespassed against [us]
2019: archdiocese of guam files bankruptcy
to settle clergy sex abuse cases
& lead [us] not into molestation
& deliver [us] from evil
men

[gapgap : tacca leontopetaloides]

ginen **family trees**

~

tåta never showed me
endangered hayun lågu   : *fire tree serianthes nelsonii*

the last mother tree
struggling to survive
in litekyan
its only home

@prutehilitekyan

"don't worry"
the military tells [us]

"we'll erect a fence
around it"

they call this "mitigation"

        yet why
does it feel like the disturbed   edge

                                                    of extinction

39

~

ekungok i trongkon yoga' calls [us]   : *stand tall*

ekungok i trongkon lemmai calls   : *open arms*

        ekungok i trongkon nunu   : *link hands*

            ekungok i trongkon ifit   : *be firm*

        ekungok i trongkon niyok   : *never break*

ekungok i halom tåno'   : *surround our last mother tree*

      & *chant*   : "[we] are the seeds

of i håyun lågu   [we] are the seeds of i håyun lågu

[we] are the seeds of the last fire tree

        ahe'   *no*

      [we] do not   *give you*

            permission"

        [gasusu : colubrina asiatica]

ginen **achiote**

~

when i close
my eyes

i see you
wearing a floral
muʻumuʻu
standing beneath
banana trees
planted
in your backyard
long before
i was born

green hands
of sagging
clusters raised
to the sky
in prayer

purple hearts
opening

[hagun admagoso : momordica charantia]

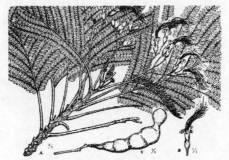

Fig. 47. Serianthes nelsonii.

"Ancestral and daily are synonyms"
—James Baldwin, from *The Evidence of Things Not Seen* (1985)

ginen **sounding lines**

~

hasso' second map   fifteen islands

vertical   crescent   i

recognize guam

southernmost & largest

read northern names

"rota aguijan tinian

saipan farallon de medinilla

anatahan sarigan guguan

alamagan pagan agrihan

asuncion maug &

farallon de pajaros"

our archipelago :

i sinahi

[hale kulales : abrus precatorius]

44

ginen **ta(là)ya**
for grandpa raphael reyes

basso' when you taught me how to weave *talàya*   in your apartment   fairfield california 2008

"*i was fifteen years old when japanese bombed guam*   *feast of   immaculate conception   december 8 1941*"

"imagine threads suspended from ceiling hooks" you tell me

"*during mass we heard airplanes & explosions so we ran home*"

"ends knotted with weights"

"*few days later we were ordered to go to plaza de españa   i saw japanese flag*"

"hold nicho & nasa around your fingers like this   atan"

[*masigsig : callicarpa candicans*]

45

ginen **mannginge'**
for ninu (godfather) diego luis duenas mendiola

~

[we]: "gi na'an
i tata i lahi-na
yan i espiritu santo åmen"

> *si yu'us ma'ase' ninu*
> *for being at my baptism*
> *on rota decades ago åmen*

[we]: "manhongge yo'
as yu'us tåta ni todo ha' hana'sina
na hanahuyong i langet yan i tåno' åmen"

> *si yu'us ma'ase' ninu*
> *for giving me chenchule'*
> *on my birthdays & graduations åmen*

[we]: "manhongge yo'
gi espiritu sånto
hu hongge
i komunon de los såntos
i ma'asi'en i isao i lina'la' tataotao ta'lo
yan i taihinekkok na bida åmen"

> *si yu'us ma'ase' ninu*
> *for feeding me*
> *five varieties of kelaguen*
> *four different grilled meats & fish*
> *two styles of fina'denne'*
> *& red rice whenever i visited åmen*

ginen **ta(là)ya**

"mesh size depends on what fish you're hunting"

"smaller for the manahak larger for the ti'ao"

"that's why [we] call the mesh *eyes*"

his hands begin to   cramp   looks at them   surprised they are empty   : *taya*

"they gave us white cloth with japanese writing pinned by our heart"

"they made us bow"

"i worked for two years in forced labor camps   soldiers came early morning"

"we built airstrip in barrigada   bayonets in our backs"

ginen **mannginge'**

~

[we]: "tatan-måmi ni gaige hao gi langet u matuna i na'ån-mu
u mamila' i gobietno-mu umafa'finas i pinto'-mu
asi gi tåno' komu gi langet"

si yu'us ma'åse' ninu
for talking story about
your tåta building model outrigger canoes
your nåna gathering åmot åmen

[we]: "nå'i ham på'go nu i kkada ha'åni na agon-måmi
ya un asi'e ham nu i diben-måmi
taiguihi i in asisi'e i dumidibi ham siha
ya cha'-mu ham pumopo'lo na in fanbasnak gi tentasion
lao na'fanlibre ham gi tailayi"

si yu'us ma'åse' ninu
for speaking chamoru
even when I didn't understand
& for translating
tåhdong meanings åmen

[we]: "si yu'us un ginegue maria bula hao gråsia
si yu'us gaige gi i ya hågu
matuna hao entre todus i famalao'an
ya matuna i finanagu-mu as jesus"

si yu'us ma'åse' ninu
for tending your farm in inalåhan
for sharing the harvest
for teaching [us] inafa'maolek
for connecting [us] to i tåno' åmen

ginen **ta(là)ya**

"they only gave us one cup of uncooked rice after work   that was our lunch every day"

"you have to imagine the threads"

"in asan we constructed machine gun encampments"

you stand in the kitchen holding your invisible talåya

"first we made forms   mixed salt water with cement & sand   then foundation"

"imagine this is the shore & sun is over there"   his eyes watery from cataracts

"i never carved my initials into concrete   i didn't want to leave fingerprints"

"make your shadow small   walk through the tides   *like this*"

49

ginen **mannginge'**

[we]: "sånta maria nånan yu'us
tayuyuti ham
man isao på'go
yan i oran i finatai-måmi"

si yu'us ma'åse' ninu
for teaching [us] minetgot
not because you were in the special forces
not because you survived vietnam
but because decades later
you fought for veteran benefits
denied to so many of our people åmen

[we]: "matuna i tåta
yan i lahina
yan i espiritu sånto
taiguihi i tutuhon-na
yan på'go
yan siempre
yan i manaihinekkok
na ha'åni
åmen"

si yu'us ma'åse' ninu
for always being my tåta's pari'
your brotherhood
taught me the true meaning
of inågofli'e' åmen

50

ginen ta(lå)ya

"after war i went to live with my brother in vallejo california   where i finished high school"

you point to the linoleum floor   "read the water currents & shadows"

"then i moved to palm springs after graduation to live with my uncle & work in his cabinet shop for two years"

"throw talåya *like this*

here now you try"

"i returned home to attend university of guam & study graphic arts"

"in 1948 i enlisted in air force   served for twenty years"

51

ginen **mannginge'**

[we]: "o jesus-hu asi'e' ham nu i isao-mami
na fanlibre ham gi guafen sasalaguan
konne tody i anti guatu gi langet
espesiatmente ayu i mas munesisita i mina'ase'-mu"

si yu'us ma'ase' ninu
for proving chamoru men
can express guinaiya amen

[we]: "sånta maria tayuyute ham
sånta ni i fuma'någo si yu'us
nånan i yiniusan na gråsia
nånan i mina'huyong I langet yan i tåno'
nånan i mina-fanlibre hit"

si yu'us ma'ase' ninu
for flying to maui for my wedding
which reminded you of rota amen

[we]: "espehos i tininas
fina'tåchong i tiningo
nina'mamago-måmi"

si yu'us ma'ase' ninu
for the toast you gave
after several budweisers
which kept going & going
& going amen

52

ginen ta(lå)ya

threads of memory weighted by your words

"in 1970s   i returned home again to work for guam department of parks & recreation"

i write the tides currents & shadows of lenguahhi

"I became first chamoru superintendent of the war in the pacific national historical park"

i weave this net   *like this*

"it was strange   my job was to preserve military structures i was forced to build"

i cast our talåya

                    to sea   to see

53

ginen **mannginge'**

[we]: "sahguan yini'usan
sahguan gef atanon
mimisterio na rosa"

si yu'us ma'åse' ninu
for planting coconut trees in mochong
for all your godchildren
when [we] were born åmen

[we]: "ekungok ham asaina"

si yu'us ma'åse' ninu
the trees are still rooted åmen

[we]: "ekungok ham asaina"

si yu'us ma'åse' ninu
for watching over [us] even now åmen

[we]: "ekungok ham asaina"

[we] bow our heads to you
[we] nginge'
& baptize your body
in our tears åmen

[we]: "tayuyute ham
na måhgong ni' taihinekok minahgong-na asaina
ya ti mamatai na mina'lak u inina åmen"

[1947-2018]
[bitbena : heliotropium indicum]

54

ginen ta(lå)ya

"tell our stories" you say. "no one can take our stories away from us"

[1926-2015]
[masigsig : callicarpa candicans]

ginen **achiote**

~

bingo is not indigenous to guam
yet here [we] are

in the air-conditioned community center
next to the village catholic church

i help set the bingo cards
& ink daubers on the cafeteria table

you sit in a wheelchair
like an ancient sea turtle

this has been your daily ritual
but the last time i played bingo with you

was 25 years ago when i was a teenager
& still lived on-island

hasso' when you won you never shouted
"bingo" too boastfully

when you lost you simply said
"agupa' *tomorrow* we'll be lucky"

here no one punishes you
for speaking chamoru

here no war invades & occupies life
no soldiers force you to bow

to a distant emperor or pledge
allegiance to a violent flag

bingo balls turn in the wire cage
like large beads from broken rosaries

i no longer attend mass
yet *here* i am praying

to the patron saint of bingo
please call your fateful combination

of letters & numbers
i pray for you to win not for money

but because you carry
so much loss

having outlived grandpa
& all your childhood friends

suddenly someone shouts "bingo"
you put down the ink dauber

sink into the shell of your wheelchair
"when's your flight" you ask me

"agupa' grandma *tomorrow*"
but today i feel so lucky

for this chance
to play bingo with you

one
last time

Rose Beatrice Hughes Perez, familian
"Talan" (Untalan) of Toto-Barrigada,
died March 31 at age of 96. Mass of
Intention is being said daily at 12:10 p.m.
at Saint Fidelis Friary in Agana Heights.
Last respects will be held from 9 to 11:15
a.m. April 20 at Immaculate Heart of
Mary Catholic Church in Toto. Mass for
Christian Burial is being said at noon.
Interment will follow at Guam Memorial
Park in Leyang, Barrigada.

[1921-2018]
[luluhot : maytenus thompsonii]

ginen **sourcings** *[burial map]*

haputo måguak finegayan
us marine corps base camp blaz
northern guåhan
under construction : desecration 2020

[to'lang]

ancient   burials

[to'lang]

dis-   turbed

[to'lang]

adult   skeleton

[to'lang]

cra   -dling

[to'lang]

child   spine

[to'lang]

how   many

[to'lang]

re-   *moved*

                              [to'lang]

o saina   *katiyi*

                    o taotaomo'na

                    potne

i militat   *amerikanu*

ginen **during your lifetime**
for guam's "greatest generation"

~

you survived
violent occupation
& the bloody march
to manenggon
you endured
the wounds of
our island stitched
by barbed wire fences
you said goodbye
to your children
as they donned uniforms
& deployed overseas
you prayed
as cancer diseased
half our relatives
you listened
as english endangered
i fino' chamoru
& snakes silenced
native birds
o saina
i doubt if [we]
will ever receive
true reparations
or sovereignty over
our own nation
i can't count
how many more
body bags will arrive
with tough boxes
& folded flags

61

i don't know if
all your children
grandchildren
great-grandchildren
& great-great-grandchildren
will ever return
guma'
during your lifetime
to show
the abundance
that you
will be
survived by

Fig. 65. Hibiscus tiliaceus.

So what's the problem with the
Brown Tree Snake in Guam??

Transporting to other islands (not on purpose)

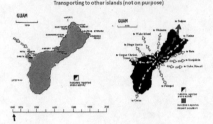

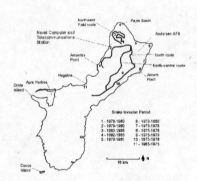

ginen **sounding lines**

~

hasso' third map
       "micro means small"
           tåta tells me "nesia means islands"

two thousand dots scattered   across the western pacific

      "here's [us]   marianas

there's palau

                yap

                      chuuk

     pohnpei
            kosrae

                     marshalls

       nauru

          & kiribati"

  "remember   we're all cousins"

[gaogao uchan : phyllanthus marianas]

ginen **the micronesian kingfisher**

~

i halom tåno'   : *deep jungle*
behind grandma's house

                              avian silence

1944: first brown tree snakes arrive on guam as stowaways aboard us military ships carrying equipment & salvaged war material from military bases in papua new guinea

~

in elementary school
[we] color pictures of
the micronesian kingfisher   : [sihek]

black beak
blue tail
green wings
orange & white feathers

native bird   i
never saw in the wild

1953: first written evidence of brown tree snakes in apra harbor area most likely introduction site on guam sightings of snakes are referred to as rumor

~

american zookeepers
arrived in the 1980s
captured 29 of the last wild
[sihek] on guam
& shipped them off-island
to safety

~

[we] memorize & recite
its scientific name
halcyon cinnamomina cinnamomina

1960s: snakes are reported throughout southern & central guam by civilians & military personnel

~

enclosure

exterior features :
quarter inch plywood
screened mesh front

interior : ceiling foam rubber
& burlap stuffed with straw

external minimum size :
nine inch by nine inch

internal height :
ten inches
between floor
& ceiling padding

cage size
for breeding pairs :
ten feet by eight feet by ten feet

~

[we] practice spelling
"endangered" & "extinct"

learn prefixes
"ex-" & "en-"

study for
vocabulary quiz

what follows your flag what snakes follow your flag what invasions follow your flag

~

eve-
ry
ch
-ick
is
ex-
treme
-ly
pre-
c
(ar)
-ious

~

[we] build fake nests
with twigs from the playground
torn paper & glue

~

"micronesian kingfishers are
notoriously difficult to breed
& they don't always properly
care for their eggs"

2010: mated pair of micronesian kingfishers laid two fertile eggs this spring inside hollowed-out palm log in special breeding room of chicago lincoln park. zoo bird house parents incubated & hatched one egg in hollow log keepers took other egg which hatched few days later inside incubation machine in lab which mimics conditions of nest

~

[we] place plastic
easter eggs in the center
of our nests

~

during incubation
keepers
track chick's
development
by shining light
through eggshell

1968: snakes have spread throughout island confirmed at northernmost area of ritidian point

"candling"

[ahgao : premna obtusifolia]

71

ginen **sounding lines**

a

r   c   h   i

p   e   l

a   g   o   e

s   r   e   s   e   m

b   l   e   c   o

n   s   t   e   l   l

a   t   i   o

n   s

[binalo : thespesia populnea]

ginen **the micronesian kingfisher**

~

after twenty days
tiny egg
begins wiggling
& cracking
until chick
emerges

at smithsonian
conservation
biology institute
in virginia *[2019]*

bird populations noticed
1970s-80s: snake population continues to grow exponentially with reports coming in from across island declining

less than
one inch long
8.5 grams

pink
featherless
female

73

~

camera
inside
incubator
captures
moment
chick
hatches

view
video
online

1981: brown tree snake found in customs area of honolulu airport having hitched its way from guam second snake discovered near aircraft hangar at barbers point naval air station

~

chick
born
eyes
closed

~

without birds
thousands of
butterflies
emerge from
cocoons [2019]

1984: most native forest birds on guam were virtually extinct when listed as threatened or endangered by us
fish and wildlife service

~

butterflies search for nectar
in flower blossoms on trees
at the war in the pacific
national historical park

[dadangse ahgaga : urena lobata]

75

~

mapmakers
named
our part of the ocean   "micronesia"
     because they viewed
        our islands & cultures
as small & insignificant

     small enough to be colonized by
spain britain germany japan australia new zealand & usa

small enough to become
     plantations church missions military bases
nuclear testing grounds detention centers scientific laboratories
      & tourist destinations

small enough to be extracted for
     souls phosphate tuna sugar copra labor
       soldiers lands & waters

small enough to be *invaded occupied diseased*
     territorialized divided bombed annexed & militarized

small enough
   to disappear
under rising
seas

[tumatis chaka : physalis angulata]

ginen **the micronesian kingfisher**

~

[we] draw timelines on poster boards

day 1 : blind & naked

day 2 : casts produced

day 5 : flight feather tracts visible on wings

day 7 : feather tracts visible on back sides & head

day 10 : eyes open   : *atan*

day 13 : feathers begin breaking through skin

day 19 : breast feathers breaking from sheaths

day 20 : skin completely covered by pin feathers

day 27 : feathers emerge from sheaths

day 29 : perching

day 30 : fully feathered

day 35 : fledging

~

keepers feed
chick
every two hours
between 6 am & 6 pm
thawed mice
mealworms
crickets
lizards

1993: brown tree snake makes its way to continental us for first time discovered in crate of household goods en route from guam delivered to ingleside naval station north side corpus christi bay texas

keepers feed
chick
with tweezers
protruding beneath
beak of
oversized kingfisher
hand puppet

without birds
guam has forty times
more spiders
than other islands

1986: brown tree snake discovered on ship carrying naval cargo as it anchored off island of diego garcia major military base in indian ocean strong probability this snake was stowaway from stopover in guam

spiderwebs
ensnare
i halom tåno'

~

[we] listen
to audio tape
of [sihek]

mimic

its song

what follows "kshh-shshh-shshh krroo-ee krroo-ee krroo-ee," your flus

~

keepers
place mirrors
in incubator
& play [sihek]
vocalizations
to prevent
chick
from imprinting
on humans

nativ

      tre s

           disap-

                thin

                  -ni

        ope   n

can

        -opy

2010: its department of agriculture "bombed" guam with dead frozen mice laced with acetaminophen lethal in snakes

                fract-

                      g ps

un-

      ger   m

            -inat d

                  see

                    -ds

~

"when birds
removed from
entire ecosystem

what follows your flag what invades what your flag disappears

guam becomes
our natural
laboratory"

~

male [sihek]
died today   *[2017]*
at smithsonian
national zoo's
bird house
in washington dc

he was 17 years old

patches contain 14,000 snakes per square mile biggest snake concentration in the world
us department of agriculture traps 6,000 brown tree snakes each year yet still two million on island most dense

approximately 140
micronesian kingfishers
are alive today

descended from
the last 29 wild birds
taken into captivity
during the 1980s

~

will guam
ever be safe
enough
to re-wild
native
birdsong

[adbahakat : ocimum sanctum]

ginen **sounding lines**

small enough
to hide
the crimes
of empire

[*alaihai : ipomoea pes-caprae brasiliensis*]

85

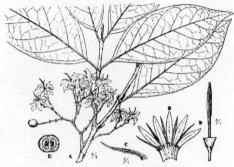

Fig. 97. Randia cochinchinensis.

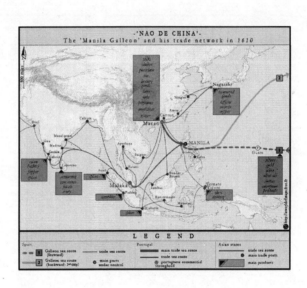

ginen **sounding lines** *[gastro-map aka the holy trinity of canned meats*
aka the chamoru food pyramid aka the micronesian triangle]

Spam

Vienna Sausage   Corned Beef

ginen **the balutan archives**

~

hasso'
tåta mixes
diced onions
donne'
cherry tomatoes
lemon juice
& soy sauce
in a bowl

"behold
fina'denne'"
he jokes   "chamoru holy water"

~

i once asked him
"who's kikkoman"

        in his myth-making voice he bellows
"kikko is an ancient chamoru chief
        who once caught 10,000 green sea turtles
& stored their tears in bottles

soy is a magic bean
that grows in the far east
turtles eat them
before swimming here"

~

i stare
at the kikkoman bottle
on our dining table

red cap
rising sun

hasso'
nakajima ki-84 hayate
fighter jets
bombing guam
december 8 1941

yet where the greater east asia
co-prosperity sphere failed
the greater east asia amino acids
concentration sphere conquered
our stomachs continue to bow
to the fifth taste of umami
& the sixth taste of empire

[golundrina : euphorbia hirta]

ginen **the zen of spam**
　　　　towards spamscendence

　　　　～

when you eat spam
what are you
eating

　　　　　　　　　　　　　　　　～

　　　　　　　　　　　　　　there is no path
　　　　　　　　　　　　　　to spam
　　　　　　　　　　　　　　spam is the path

　　　　　～

what is the sound
of no spam
frying

　　　　　　　　[jatbas babui : blechum brownei]

~

the transparent tear-drop
         shaped bottle designed
by kenji ekuan in 1961

as a child he witnessed
the atomic bombing of hiroshima
his sister died in explosion
his dad from cancer

"everything became nothing"
he once said
"we need to bring back
material things to human life"

after 100 prototypes
he arrived at its final form

"this shape is so gentle
during war we were forced
         to act differently

but for 1,000 years
the history of japanese people
was very gentle"

~

"if soy sauce is japanese"
i ask my tåta
"what makes fina'denne' chamoru?"

"it's chamoru" he says
"because [we] made it our own"

      he

           tilts

               the

                  bottle

                  until

                    it

                  bows

                    to

                     us

[amot tumaga : cassia sp]

93

ginen **the zen of spam**
towards spamvana

~

what is
the true
taste
of spam

~

spam is
the absence
of striving
for spam

~

does a poem
have spam nature

[tumatas chaka : physalis sp.]

94

ginen **the legends of juan malo**
[the origin of tabasco]

Guam is considered the Tabasco capital of the world. On average, each Chamoru consumes 4 ounces of Tabasco each year, which is more per capita than any other country! My Authentic Indigenous Grandpa used to joke that Tabasco was Chamoru cologne ("Eau de Pika"). My Authentic Indigenous Grandma called Tabasco, "Chamoru åmot." Whenever I felt sick she made Tabasco tea. For skin burns, snake bites, rashes, or muscle aches, she exclaimed: "Just Tabasco it!" My Authentic Indigenous Dad inherited this spicy legacy and baptized all his food in Tabasco. When he initiated me into the Tabasco condiment cult, he proclaimed: "The President of the United States, The Queen of England, and even astronauts at the International Space Station all love Tabasco!" When I asked him, "Where does Tabasco come from?" He said: "The Legend of the Origin of Tabasco has been passed down for generations. As told to me, there was an ancient Chamoru chief named Maga'lahi Donne' who lived during the Great Famine. To save our people from dying of bland taste, he boarded his canoe and sailed beyond the tenth horizon. After a year at sea, he spotted an island made of salt. Ghosts on canoes surrounded the island, whispering: 'Remember the Atakapa-Ishak.' When he reached the island, an Authentic White Man named McIlhenny welcomed him. Together they watched migrant workers pick the finest Tabasco peppers. The seeds were then mailed to farmers in Mexico, Guatemala, Honduras, Columbia, Ecuador, Peru, South Africa, Zambia, Zimbabwe, and Mozambique. McIlhenny said: 'Now we wait.'"

ginen **the balutan archives**
    re-heating gertrude stein

Ekungok!
I'm no fool.
I know that in daily life
[we] don't go around saying
Calrose is Calrose is Calrose is Calrose.
Yes, I'm no fool,
but I think that in that line
the rose is red
rice
for the first time
in English poetry.

[pupulu : piper beetle]

~

"Nine months later, bright red peppers arrived in the mail. The peppers were then ground into a mash & stored with salt in oak barrels. Maga'lahi Donne' passed the time with self-guided tours of the wildlife refuge, ancient salt mine, secretive seed vault, historical museum, reasonably priced gift shop, restaurant & participatory cooking classes. At night, he contemplated the translation of the word, *Tabasco,* as *flooded land.* Three years later, the mash was finally strained, mixed with vinegar & bottled. McIlhenny gave Maga'lahi Donne' a case of Tabasco & said, 'Return home. Save your people.' That is how Tabasco arrived to Guam." After he finished reciting this legend, my dad opened a can of Tabasco-flavored SPAM called "Hot & Spicy SPAM" specially formulated for Guam. Ingredients: Pork with Ham, Mechanically Separated Chicken, Water, Salt, Modified Potato Starch, Sugar, Sodium Phosphates, Potassium Chloride, TABASCO® Brand Dry Red Flavoring (Red Pepper, Distilled Vinegar, Salt), Sodium Ascorbate, Oleoresin of Paprika, Sodium Nitrite. I will always eat it.

[asiga : sodium chloride]

ginen **the zen of spam**
     towards spamlightenment

  ~

first there is spam
then there is no spam
then there is

       ~

      is america
      spam

  ~

"why aren't you
eating spam"
you ask me

"i no longer see spam
as outside"
i reply

"why eat"

[*llana niyok : cocos nucifera*]

98

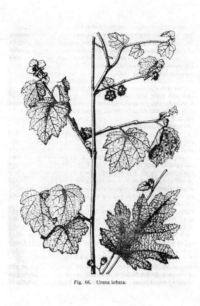

Fig. 66. Urena lobata.

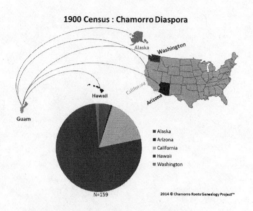

1900 Census : Chamorro Diaspora

Alaska
Washington
California
Arizona
Hawaii
Guam

- Alaska
- Arizona
- California
- Hawaii
- Washington

N=159

2014 © Chamorro Roots Genealogy Project™

Chamorro Diaspora in the U.S.

Legend:
Data Classes

	126 - 1287
	1447 - 3056
	3407 - 6647
	10167 - 14829
	44425 - 44425

TOP 10

California	44,425
Washington	14,829
Texas	10,167
Hawaii	6,647
Florida	5,904
Nevada	5,512
Arizona	4,276
Georgia	3,856

2010 Census
Source: US Census Bureau

2015 Bernard Punzalan | Chamorro Roots Genealogy Project™

ginen **sounding lines**

~

hasso' fourth map
pacific ocean rimmed

by asia   america

countless archipelagoes divided

"this is polynesia   poly means many"
tåta traces a triangle between
hawai'i

easter island (rapa nui)   new zealand (aotearoa)

then he draws an imaginary circle
around papua new guinea solomon islands fiji
vanuatu & new caledonia
"this is melanesia   mela means black"

"remember we're all relatives"

[bingan aggak : pandanus tectorius]

ginen **aerial roots** *[off-island chamorus]*

~

[1995]

hasso' the entrance
to guam international airport
resembles i sakman   : *outrigger canoe*

"flying proa"
because it swiftly skimmed
waves

[we] wait
at the gate
talk story with relatives
take pictures
hug
wave goodbye

[we] board
i batkon aire   : *air boat*

one-way flight
on *continental*

the name
of our airlines

the name
of our destination

~

hasso' first day
at my new high school in california
the homeroom teacher asks
"where are you from"

     "the mariana islands"
     i answer

"i've never heard of that place"
        he replies "prove it exists"

yet when i step in front of the world map on the classroom wall
        it transforms into a mirror :

the pacific ocean   like my body
split   in two
& flayed   to the margins
                  i

find australia   philippines   japan

       then point to the empty space between
          "i'm from this invisible archipelago"

my classmates laugh   & even though i descend from
      oceanic navigators   i feel so lost

shipwrecked   on the coast
of a strange   continent

~

"are you a citizen"
the teacher probes

"yes
my island guam
is us territory"
i explain

> [we] *attend american schools*
> *eat american food*
> *listen to american music*
> *watch american movies*
> *play american sports*
> *learn american history*
> *dream american dreams*
> & *die in american wars*
>
> : *what follows your flag*

"you speak english well"
he proclaims

"with almost no accent"

& isn't that what it means
to be   a diasporic chamoru

to feel *foreign*
in a domestic sense

[hale nunu : ficus prolixa]

ginen **åmot**
[100 healing rituals for chamorus suffering from homesickness & diaspora]

1. Open a can of Spam. Follow your instincts home.
2. Make fina'denne' & baptize everything in it.
3. Call your Chamoru grandparent(s) & ask them for stories about guma'.
4. Read *Pacific Daily News* online.
5. YouTube Jesse Manibusan's song "Forever Chamorro."
6. Build an altar using shells, coral, postcards & photos.
7. Find your family in *Chamorro Roots Genealogy Project*.
8. Read *Guampedia* online.
9. Open a can of Vienna Sausages & a Budweiser. Call that breakfast.
10. Google Earth your village.
11. YouTube Jesse & Ruby's song "Guam take me back." Follow their voices home.
12. Make kadun pika, even if you live in Arizona.
13. Call your Chamoru parent(s) & ask them for stories about guma'.
14.
15. Close your eyes & imagine the most beautiful sunset you've ever seen.
16. Open a can of Corned Beef. Cook two eggs, any style. Eat with two scoops white rice & fina'denne'. Call that brunch.
17. Read Michael Lujan Bevacqua's blog.
18. Lather coconut oil over everything.
19. Read *Hale-ta* book series. Follow our roots home.
20. Sport your Fokai, Crowns, or Magas apparel!
21. Call your Chamoru godparent(s) & ask them for stories about guma'.
22. Tell your non-Chamoru friends taotaomo'na stories. Tell your Chamoru friends how your non-Chamoru friends don't understand taotaomo'na stories.
23. Read Faye Untalan's dissertation "An Exploratory Study of Island Migrations: Chamorros of Guam" (1984).
24. YouTube K.C. DeLeon Guerrero's song, "Kustumbren Chamoru." Dance your way home.
25.

26. Buy the Chamorro-English dictionary. Hold on to that moment when you open it for first time. Learn one new word of our language everyday. Hold each word carefully, as if your hands were nests for endangered birds.

[binag niyok : cocos nucifera]

ginen **aerial roots**

~

  over the last fifty years
chamorus have migrated
to escape the violent memories of war
    to seek jobs schools hospitals adventure & love
but most of all to serve in the military
deployed & stationed to bases
around the world

according to the 2010 census

    44,000 chamorus live in california
    15,000 in washington
    10,000 in texas
    7,000 in hawai'i
    & 70,000 more in every other state
    even puerto rico

[we] are the most "geographically

                                        dispersed"

pacific islander population within the united
        states & off-island chamorus now outnumber
our on-island kin   with generations having been born
        away from our ancestral homelands
                including my daughters

~

some of [us] will be able to return home
　　　　for holidays weddings & funerals
　　　　　　　others won't be able to afford
　　　　expensive plane tickets
to the western pacific

years &
decades will pass
between trips
& each visit
will feel too short

[we] will lose
contact
with family & friends　　　　　　& our islands will continue
　　　　　　　　　　　　　　　to change
　　　　　　　　　　　　　　　until they become
　　　　　　　　　　　　　　　unfamiliar

& isn't that too
what it means to be
a diasporic chamorus

to feel *foreign*
in your own homeland

~

even after more than 25 years away
there are still times i feel adrift
        without itinerary or destination

when i wonder   what if [we] stayed

        what if [we] return

when the undertow
of these questions pull   [us] out to sea

        remember   migration flows through our blood
                            like the subaerial roots
                            of banyan trees

        hasso'   our ancestors taught [us] how to carry
                            culture in the canoes
                            of our bodies

        remember   our people
                            scattered like stars
                            form new constellations
                            when [we] gather

        hasso'   home is not simply a house
                            village or island

        home is   *an archipelago of belonging*

[hagun pago : hibiscus tiliaceus]

109

25. Make hineksa' aga'ga'.

27. In order to make hineksa' aga'ga', you'll need to buy achiote. Drive to the closest Asian grocery store. Look for Mama Sita's powdered achiote from Philippines, which comes in thin yellow packets. Remember your grandma's red-stained hands after she harvested achiote seeds from her yard.

28. Join Facebook groups "Chamorro Events Worldwide" and "Faces of Chamorro Diaspora."

29. Read Tanya Taimanglo's book *Attitude 13: A Daughter of Guam's Collection of Short Stories.*

30. Go for hikes that end in waterfalls. Close your eyes & call these places guma'.

31. Chew the pugua you've been saving in the freezer.

32. Buy round-trip tickets home for a holiday, wedding, christening, graduation, or funeral. Worry about credit card debt later.

33. Listen to "Beyond the Fence" podcast online through KPRG Public Radio Guam.

34. Wear your Chamoru bracelets & let them clang like your mom, aunties, and grandmas used to.

35. Bump JD Crutch's song "Bente Uno" really loud on your morning drive to work.

36. Date a fellow diasporic Chamoru who can relate to your experience (make sure you aren't actually related before going on second date).

37. Listen to Dakota Alcantara-Camacho's song, "Where you From," on his All Life is Sacred EP on Soundcloud.

38. Visit the Spam Museum in Austin, Minnesota.

39. After the Spam Museum, visit The Herbivorous Butchershop in Minneapolis, Minnesota, the first ever vegan butcher shop, which was founded by two diasporic Chamorus who were banished from Guam for being vegetarians.

40. Play bingo.

41. Fanginge' every Chamoru elder you meet.

42. YouTube Island Trybe's, "Blow ya Mynd." Lowride your way home!

43. Wear your Sinahi everywhere.
44. Read any book by Peter Onedera.
45. Get a Latte stone tattoo.
46.
47. Read Robert Underwood's essay, "Excursions into Inauthenticity: The Chamorros of Guam" (1985), especially the section "The Emergence of the Migrant Stream."
48. YouTube Erica Nalani Benton's song, "Back to Guåhan."
49. Buy Chamoru language children's book from the University of Guam Press & from The Guam Bus. Imagine your parents reading this book to you when you were young.
50. Cha-cha-cha everywhere.

[hagun dago : dioscorea alata]

ginen **family trees** *[i tronkon niyok]*

~

on September 11 2007
in lower tumon
detected on guam
native to southeast asia
a large scarab beetle
the coconut rhinoceros beetle [crb]

once
i bought a can
of coconut water
for my tåta
in california

after the first taste
he can't stop talking story

about his tropical past :

"as a barefoot child
i climbed coconut trees
that touched the clouds

during each generation
of 3,000%
there will be a population increase
& 100% survival rate
with 50% sex ratio
lays 100 eggs during her lifetime
female rhino beetle

my grandpa
removed the husks
with his teeth
& cracked the shells
with his knuckles

my grandma
grated the meat
with her fingernails
& squeezed it
into milk & oil"

112

~

"those products are trendy
& expensive now"
i tell him
"imported from plantations
in sri lanka philippines
& thailand"

he says
"my great-aunties sat
in a circle weaving coconut leaves
& if you press your ear
to their woven mats
you can still hear
gossip & singing"

& because circles make memory
seem less broken

he recalls
"my great-uncles also sat
in a circle braiding
dried coconut fibers into rope
used to lash canoes
& thatch houses"

2007: an eradication program
using sanitation
an island wide network
of 2,000 pheromone traps
& pesticides fail to stop
beetle spread & growth

2010: all parts of guam
are infested by beetles
most breeding sites
are inaccessible for application
of eradication tactics
being in the deep jungle
or on military property)

[binagle : cocos nucifera]

51. If you get into trouble, blame it on the cha-cha-cha.
52. YouTube Melvin Won Pat-Borja's poem-testimony, "No Deal."
53. Drive to the nearest military base. Close your eyes & imagine Angel Santos & the entire Nasion Chamoru flying over the barbed-wire fences.
54. Recite the "Inifresi."
55. Just Tabasco everything!
56. Read Michael Perez's essay, "Pacific Identities Beyond US Racial Formation: Case of Chamorro Ambivalence and Flux" (2002).
57. YouTube Jesse Bais's song, "Guam on my Mind."
58. Make chicken kelaguen.
59. In order to make chicken kelaguen, you must first buy coconut. Drive to nearest Asian grocery store. Crack open the coconut at home only to find it is completely rotted inside. Drive back to grocery store with your machete. Argue with the owner, who won't exchange it. Go back to your car & get the machete. Walk back into produce aisle. Crack open coconuts until you find a good one. Pay for coconut, machete in hand.
60. Buy a round-trip ticket home for no reason. Worry about credit card debt later.
61. YouTube "Fanohge March."
62. Eat at a Chamoru restaurant or food truck in your area. Try not to ruin meal by comparing the food to your parents' or grandparents' cooking.
63. Recite the novena in Chamoru using the rosary your grandma gave you before you left Guam. If you can't say the novena in Chamoru, YouTube "Chamorro rosary."
64. Read Vicente Diaz's book, *Repositioning the Missionary: Rewriting the Histories of Colonialism, Native Catholicism, and Indigeneity in Guam.* Remember what our ancestors survived.
65. Give chenchule' every chance you get.
66. Visit Guma Yo'åmte, Guam's first traditional healing center.

67.

68. Get your clan name tattooed across your back.

69. Buy Manny Crisostomo's book *Legacies of Guam: I Kustumbren Chamoru.*

70. Wear your "Prutehi yan Difendi" t-shirt.

71. Close your eyes & remember the last time you hiked to Pågat.

72. Place a Guam or CNMI seal sticker on your truck & drive on the freeway until another diasporic Chamoru spots you.

73. Visit the Waikīkī Spam Jam in Honolulu, Oʻahu.

74. Read Keith Camacho's book *Cultures of Commemoration: The Politics of War, Memory, and History in the Mariana Islands.* Remember what our ancestors survived.

75. Tell yourself that you will return one day, you just have few more things to take care of out here.

76. YouTube Flora Baza Quan's song "Hagu." Hail the Queen of Chamoru music!

77. Enroll in Michael Lujan Bevacqua's free, online Chamoru language classes. With your mother tongue, slowly paddle your way home.

[chaguan kabayo : dactyloctenium aegyptium]

ginen **family trees**

~

i read aloud
the nutrition facts label
45 calories
30mg sodium
470mg potassium
11g sugar
fat & cholesterol free

he responds with this origin tale

"once
a young girl
beloved by our entire island
dies during a time of drought

her family buries her
& weeps upon the grave
from which an unfamiliar tree
sprouts

for years it grows & blooms
until a large hard nut
falls & cracks open

2011: attempts to control
beetles with biological
control agents using virus
oryctes rhinoceros
& fungus metarhizium majus fail

2014: local fishermen
use small fish gill net
called tekken
which capture 65% of
adult beetles emerging from
compost or green-waste piles

116

her mother braves
the first sip
then smiles for the first time
in years
as if her body
having been completely emptied
is finally replenished

from that harvest
our people planted a sapling
whenever a child was born

as generations passed
trees became kin
teaching [us] how to bend
without breaking
how to create without wasting
how to take
without depleting"

*2015: typhoon dolphin
generates abundant beetle
breeding sites
triggering self-sustaining
island-wide outbreak*

117

"so many
coconut trees
back home
are dying"
he says

2016: beetles have destroyed half of all coconut trees on guam

"the beetles dig
into the crown
& eat the heart"

[we] discard
empty cans
in the recycling bin
& swallow
bitter aftertaste

[tubatuba : jatropha curcas]

ginen the micronesian kingfisher

[2000]

hasso' visiting the san diego zoo
with friends from college

in the aviary
atan
black beak
blue tail
green wings
orange & white
feathers

"kshh-skshh-skshh-kroo-ee kroo-ee kroo-ee"

"håfa adai"
i whisper
into the cage

"guahu si craig
familian gollo
ginen mongmong

but i live here now
in california

like you"

~

captive-reared
[sihek]
were first flown
to the marianas
in 2003

today
ten [sihek]
live
in captivity
on guam

"kshh-skshh-skshh-kroo-ee kroo-ee kroo-ee"

"soon"
i whisper

"it'll be safe enough
for you

to return home

promise"

78. Read my poetry books (no refunds).
79. Attend the nearest Liberation Day party, which you can locate using the www.guamliberation.com website.
80. Read Laura Marie Torres Souder's *Daughters of the Island: Contemporary Chamorro Women Organizers on Guam* (1992).
81. Call any one of your Chamoru aunties and uncles. Be thankful to your grandparents for having so many children that there'll always be someone to give you stories about guma'.
82. Learn how to craft a kulo'. Blow the kulo' everywhere.
83. Read Jesi Lujan Bennett's MA thesis, "Apmam Tiempo Ti Uli'e Hit (Long Time No See): Chamorro Diaspora and the TransPacific Home."
84. YouTube Jesse Bais's song "Uno Hit." Remember that off-island & on-island Chamorus are one.
85. Get "Dandan I Paneretas" stuck in your head all December. Air stick dance with imaginary partner.
86. Attend the nearest Feast Day of Immaculate Conception & lukao your way home.
87. Subscribe to the Fanachu podcast.
88. YouTube "Malafunkshun." Laugh your way home.
89. Look at US dollar bills. Find "Gumataotao."
90. Read Lehua Taitano's poetry books, *A Bell Made of Stones* & *Inside Me An Island*.
91. Wear zoris everywhere.
92. YouTube episodes of Nihi! online. Imagine watching them with your parents when you were young.
93. Buy a one-way ticket home. Stay.
94. YouTube Johnny Sablan's song, "Nobia Nene." Dance with someone you love.
95. Read Christine Taitano DeLisle's book *Placental Politics: CHamoru Women, White Womanhood, and Indigeneity under U.S. Colonialism in Guam*. Remember what our ancestors survived.

96. Join the nearest Chamoru, Marianas, Northern Marianas, Sons and Daughters of Guam, or Hafa Adai Club in your state. If there are none, start your own Chamoru club in your church, community center, military base, high school, or university.
97. Attend the Chamorro Cultural Festival in San Diego. Call this gupot home.
98.
99. Whisper, "mahålang," the only word that can carry all our longing.
100. Drive to the ocean. Take off your shoes or zories and feel the sand between your toes. Step into the salt water. Return your tears to the sea, where they belong. Close your eyes, and call your body guma'.

[achiote : bixa orellana]

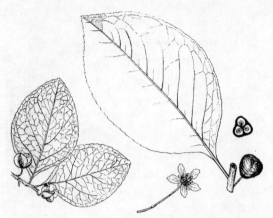

Fig. 60. Maytenus thompsonii.

"There is no world, there are only islands."
    —Jacques Derrida,
      from The Beast and the Sovereign (Volume II)

ginen **sounding lines**
    for hsinya huang

~

tåta never hung a fifth map in the hallway

        i first see it as an adult in taiwan

            "austro means south" the tour guide says

a highlighted area   in the shape of a full sail   stretches

            from madagascar to malay peninsula & indonesia

                north to philippines & taiwan

then traversing micronesia & polynesia

        "we don't know why they migrated"

                imagine four hundred million people alive today

        who speak a thousand different languages

            all descend from one

    mother tongue   one genetic family

~

read maps
closely *navigate*

     beyond the violent divisions

        of national & maritime borders

   beyond the scarred
latitudes & longitudes
 of empire

       arrive at this cartography

    of our most expansive legends

    & deepest routes

~

re

me   *mb*   *er*

pa *ci* *fic* *o*

ce *an*

is *ou*

r *bl* *ue*

co *nt* *i*

ne *nt*

127

ginen **ars pasifika**

~

i return home
        for the first time
after fifteen years away

                                          [2010]

& visit an english class
        at one of guam's
public high schools

as i read aloud
        from my new book
i notice a student
crying

"what's wrong" i ask

she says "i've never seen
        our culture
in a book before

i just thought
[we] weren't worthy

of literature"

~

how many young islanders have dived
    into the depths of

a book
only to find
    bleached coral
& emptiness

[we] were taught that missionaries
        were the first readers in the pacific
                because they could decipher
                        the strange signs of the bible
            [we] were taught that missionaries
        were the first authors
because they possessed the authority
of written words

             today
studies show that islander students
        read & write below grade level

"it's natural" experts claim
    "your ancestors
were an illiterate
oral people"

~

don't believe their claims

        our ancestors deciphered signs
             in nature
interpreted star formations & sun positions
        cloud & wind patterns
             wave currents & ocean
         efflorescence

that's why master navigator papa mau once said

      "if you can read the ocean
          you will never be lost"

~

    now let me tell you
about *pacific written traditions*

how our ancestors
    tattooed their skin
        with defiant scripts
    of intricately
inked genealogies

how they carved epics
      into hard wood
with sharpened points
    their hands
& the pressure
    & responsibility
   of memory

how they stenciled
    petroglyphic lyrics
on cave walls
    with clay
fire & smoke

~

so the next time someone tells you
    our people were illiterate

teach them
about our visual literacies

our ability to read
      the intertextual
           sacredness
       of all things

       & always remember

if [we] can write the ocean
    [we] will never be silenced

[batones : hyptis capitata]

52

MORINDA LITTORALIS.—Blanco.
MORINDA CITRIFOLIA.—Lacu.—DC.—Miq.

133

~

"Åmot" is the Chamoru word for, "medicine," and commonly refers to native or introduced plants that possess healing and medicinal qualities. In different historical periods, traditional Chamoru healers were known as yo'åmte, eåmtis, makåna, kakåhna, and suruhåna. These specialists treated illnesses with natural åmot, matantan and malasa (massage), pålai (body lotion), and madieta (dietary advice). They gathered åmot in the jungle or in their gardens, prepared the medicine, and administered to their patients. They also utilized prayers, chants, and the invocation of i taotao'mona, or ancestral spirits, in the healing process. The eåmtis tradition was displaced by the colonial intrusions of western medicine, hospitals, and doctors. The militarization of our homeland by the United States has led to the pollution of the land, the fragmentation of the jungle, and the endangerment of many native medicinal plants throughout the island, including the area of Litekyan. Today, Chamoru people suffer from high rates of colonial diseases, like cancer and diabetes. In response, a new generation of healers are revitalizing the practice of åmot from the eåmtis with whom the tradition has survived. This had led them to advocate for the protection of the environment and the health of our people.

The opening quote is a Chamoru chant that a suruhåna (medicinal healer) would make as she entered the jungle to gather herbs. Quoted in "Ancient CHamoru Medicine Making," by Dr. Marilyn Salas, published in *Guampedia*: https://www.guampedia.com/ancient-chamorro-medicine-making/. Updated December 16, 2019.

I am grateful to these sources that are referenced throughout this book:

Borja, M. (2009). *Directory of Traditional Healers and Medicinal Plants in the Commonwealth of the Northern Mariana Islands.* Intetnon Amot Natibi, Saipan, MP.

Hattori, A. (2004). *Colonial dis-ease: US Navy health policies and the Chamoru of Guam, 1898-1941.* Honolulu: University of Hawaii.

Lizama, T. (2011). *How are traditional healing practices being perpetuated and preserved in modern Guam: A Phenomenological Study.* Unpublished dissertation.

Lizama, T. (2014). "Yo'åmte: A Deeper Type of Healing Exploring The State of Indigenous Chamorro Healing Practices." *Pacific Asia Inquiry*, Volume 5, Number 1, Fall 2014, 97-106.

McMakin, P. (1978). "The Suruhanos: A traditional curer on the island of Guam in Micronesia." *Journal of the University of Guam, 14*(1), 13-67.

~

The botanical illustrations are sourced from the Flickr account of Museum Studies and Museum Consortium at the University of Hawai'i at Mānoa. Images from: Stone, Benjamin C. (1970). *The Flora of Guam: A Manual for the Identification of the Vascular Plants of the Island.* Micronesica Volume 6, University of Guam.

~

The timeline of Catholic history on Guam is sourced from the website, *The Roman Catholic Archdiocese of Agana History*. http://www.archdioceseofagana.com/aoa_history.htm.

~

Information on the brown tree snake was sourced from: Fritts, Thomas H. And Dawn Leasman-Tanner (2001). *The Brown Tree Snake on Guam: How the Arrival of One Invasive Species Damaged the Ecology, Commerce, Electrical Systems and Human Health on Guam: A Comprehensive Information Source.* U.S. Fish and Wildlife Service.

Another essential source is Wiles, Gary J., Jonathan Bart, Robert Beck,

135

and Celestino F. Aguon (2003). "Impacts of the Brown Tree Snake: Patterns of Decline and Species Persistence in Guam's Avifauna." *Conservation Biology*, Volume 17, No.5: pp. 1350-1360.

Rodda, Gordon H., Thomas H. Fritts, and Paul J. Conry (1992). "Origin and Population Growth of the Brown Tree Snake, Boiga irregularis, on Guam." *Pacific Science*, volume 46, no. 1: 46-57.

Sablan, Jerick (2019). "Lots of Butterflies sighted throughout the island." *Pacific Daily News*, August 16, 2019. https://www.guampdn.com/story/news/2019/08/16/lots-butterflies-sighted-throughout-island/2026811001/.

Rice University. "Snakes minus birds equals more spiders for Guam: Ecologists look for effects of bird loss caused by invasive brown treesnake." *Science Daily*. Science Daily, 13 September 2012. www.sciencedaily.com/releases/2012/09/120913123631.htm.

Mullen, William (2010). "One of world's most endangered species, Guam kingfishers live on in zoos in struggle to survive." *Chicago Tribune*, June 28, 2010.

Smithsonian Conservation Biology institute (2018). "Rare Guam kingfisher hatched." *Smithsonian Insider*, June 1, 2018. https://insider.si.edu/2018/06/rare-guam-kingfishers-hatches-at-conservation-biology-institute/.

Smithsonian National Zoo & Conservation Biology Institute. "Extinct in the Wild Guam Kingfisher Hatches at the Smithsonian Conversation Biology Institute." *Smithsonian National Zoo & Conservation Biology Institute* Website. April 26, 2019. https://nationalzoo.si.edu/news/extinct-wild-guam-kingfisher-hatches-smithsonian-conservation-biology-institute

Martin, Claire (2013). "Where Have the Trees of Guam Gone?" *Smithsonian Magazine*, April 11, 2013. https://www.smithsonianmag.

com/science-nature/where-have-the-trees-of-guam-gone-19756341/.

Aguon, Mindy (2017). "Kingfisher from Guam dies at Smithsonian Zoo." *The Guam Daily Post*, January 12, 2017. https://www.postguam. com/news/local/rare-guam-kingfisher-dies-at-smithsonian-zoo/ article_62d8efe8-d790-11e6-831e-efbfdb33159c.html.

~

Quotes from Kenji Ekuan are sourced from: Bever, Lindsey. (2015). "In your refrigerator, perhaps, a remembrance of Japan's most illustrious designer." *The Washington Post*, February 10, 2015. https://www. washingtonpost.com/news/morning-mix/wp/2015/02/10/kenji-ekuan-the-designer-behind-kikkomans-iconic-red-capped-soy-sauce-bottle-dies-at-85/.

~

The quote from Papa Mau is sourced from: Thompson, Nainoa (2017). "Non-Instrument Navigation." *Wayfinders: A Pacific Odyssey* Website. https://www.pbs.org/wayfinders/wayfinding2.html

~

Passages in "ta(lå)ya" are sourced from Evans-Hatch & Associates, Inc. 2004. *War in the Pacific National Historic Park: An Administrative History*. "Chapter 9: Expanding Park Operations: The Reyes Years (1983-1991)." https://www.nps.gov/parkhistory/online_books/wapa/adhi/adhi9.htm

~

Information on the Coconut Rhinoceros Beetle are sourced from the *Guam Rhinoceros Beetle Project* at the University of Guam College of Natural & Applied Sciences website. https://cnas-re.uog.edu/crb/. Especially important is Dr. Aubrey's Moore's 2017 study, "The Coconut Rhinoceros Beetle Problem on Guam: Past, Present, and Future."

137

https://aubreymoore.github.io/CRB-Guam-Past-Present-Future/.

~

Maps:

The Chamorro diaspora maps were sourced from the *Chamorro Roots Genealogy Project* Website, created by Bernard Punzalan, "The Surge: Chamorro Diaspora in the U.S." January 23, 2015 . https://www.chamorroroots.com/v7/index.php/9-taotao-tano/158-the-surge-chamorro-diaspora-in-the-us.

Gingerich, Stephen B., and Jenson, John W. (2010). *Groundwater availability study for Guam; goals, approach, products, and schedule of activities.* U.S. Geological Survey Fact Sheet 2010-3084.

"The island of Guam, in the western Pacific Ocean, has a freshwater-lens system in the productive limestone aquifer (Northern Guam Lens Aquifer) underlying the island's northern half, where most of the population resides and where population is expected to increase substantially as a result of military expansion. A groundwater-availability study will help guide sustainable management of this critical and increasingly used resource. The darker "window" in the middle of the aquifer is the extent of the volcanic basement rock above sea level, where groundwater pumping is precluded by the very low permeability of the rock. (Image from U.S. Department of Agriculture, Natural Resources Conservation Service, 20060714, Orthophoto Mosaic for Guam)."

Brown Tree snake maps are sourced from Wiles, Gary J., Jonathan Bart, Robert Beck, and Celestino F. Aguon (2003). Impacts of the Brown Tree Snake: Patterns of Decline and Species Persistence in Guam's Avifauna. Conservation Biology, Volume 17, No.5: pp. 1350-1360.

Austronesia with hypothetical greatest expansion extent per Blench, Roger (2009). "Remapping the Austronesian expansion". In Evans,

138

Bethwyn. Discovering History Through Language: Papers in Honour of Malcolm Ross. Pacific Linguistics.

Acknowledgements

Thanks to the editors of Argotist Books in England for publishing some of these poem in the chapbook, *Ekungok, Listen (2017)*. Thanks to the editors of the following journals in which some of these poems first appeared in earlier versions: *Poetry Magazine, World Literature Today, New American Writing, Bamboo Ridge: Journal of Hawaii Literature and Arts, Prairie Schooner, Cream City Review, 92nd St Y Poetry Center, The Rumpus, At Length, Dialogist, NACLA: Report on the Americas, Resist Much/Obey Little: Inaugural Poems to the Resistance, The Lifted Brow* (Australia), *Rabbit: A Journal of Nonfiction Poetry* (Australia), *Shima: International Journal of Island Studies* (Australia), *Wasafiri: International Contemporary Writing* (England), *Zin Daily* (Croatia), *IKA Literary Journal* (Aotearoa/New Zealand), *Capilano Literary Review* (Canada).

Thanks to Guam Educators Symposium on Soil and Water Conservation conference in 2016 for commissioning the poem,"ginen family trees [litekyan]."

Audio version of some of these poems can also be found in my spoken word poetry album, *Crosscurrent (2017)*, available on Bandcamp.

Dr. Craig Santos Perez is an indigenous Chamoru from the Pacific Island of Guåhan (Guam). He is the co-editor of six anthologies and the author of five poetry collections and the monograph, Navigating Chamoru Poetry: Indigeneity, Aesthetics, and Decolonization (University of Arizona Press, 2022).

He earned an MFA in Creative Writing from the University of San Francisco and a Ph.D. in Comparative Ethnic Studies from the University of California, Berkeley. He is a full professor in the English department, and an affiliate faculty with the Center for Pacific Islands Studies and the Indigenous Politics Program, at the University of Hawai'i, Mānoa. He teaches creative writing, Pacific literature, and eco-poetry.

He has received the American Book Award, Pen Center USA/Poetry Society of America Literary Prize, Hawai'i Literary Arts Council Award, Nautilus Book Award, and the George Garrett Award for Outstanding Community Service in Literature from AWP. He has also received fellowships and grants from the Lannan, Ford, and Mellon Foundations, as well as from the American Council of Learned Societies and the Modern Language Association.

from unincorporated territory
[åmot]
by Craig Santos Perez
Cover art by Craig Santos Perez
Interior typefaces: Garamond and Garamond Premier Pro

Cover design by Craig Santos Perez
Interior design by Craig Santos Perez and Laura Joakimson

Printed in the United States
by Books International, Dulles, Virginia
On 55# Glatfelter B19 Antique 360 ppi
(for books over 100 pages use:) On Glatfelter 50# Cream Natures Book
440 ppi
Acid Free Archival Quality Recycled Paper

Publication of this book was made possible in part by gifts from
Katherine & John Gravendyk in honor of Hillary Gravendyk,
Francesca Bell, Mary Mackey, and The New Place Fund

Omnidawn Publishing
Oakland, California
Staff and Volunteers, Spring 2023
Rusty Morrison, senior editor & publisher
Laura Joakimson, executive director
Rob Hendricks, poetry & fiction, & post-pub marketing
Sharon Zetter, poetry editor & book designer
Jeffrey Kingman, copy editor
Liza Flum, poetry editor
Anthony Cody, poetry editor
Jason Bayani, poetry editor
Gail Aronson, fiction editor
Jennifer Metsker, marketing assistant
Sophia Carr, marketing assistant